# PDCA

Project Execution Essentials Handbook

Sumeet Savant

# DEDICATION

To all Lean Six Sigma enthusiasts and practitioners.

# CONTENTS

# ACKNOWLEDGMENT

Special thanks to my wife Sahana, for always supporting me in all my endeavors and to the exciting world of Lean Six Sigma for accepting me and providing me a platform to perform on a global scale.

# ABOUT THE AUTHOR

Sumeet Savant is a Lean Six Sigma Master Black Belt Mentor and coach, with more than a decade of experience in executing, leading and mentoring Lean Six Sigma process improvement projects. He is a BTech, MBA, and Prince certified Practitioner. He has facilitated hundreds of process improvement projects, and coached hundreds of professionals, Yellow, Green, and Black Belts over the years. He lives in Mumbai, India with his family.

# LEAN SIX SIGMA PROJECT EXECUTION ESSENTIALS SERIES

**H**andbooks that will help execute a variety of Lean Six Sigma projects,

- PDCA: Project Execution Essentials Handbook
- DMAIC: Project Execution Essentials Handbook
- DMADV: Project Execution Essentials Handbook
- DMADOV: Project Execution Essentials Handbook
- Lean Action Workout: Project Execution Essentials Handbook
- Lean DMAIC: Project Execution Essentials Handbook
- Lean DMADV: Project Execution Essentials Handbook
- Lean DMADOV: Project Execution Essentials Handbook

# PURPOSE OF WRITING THIS BOOK

With businesses around the world focusing on delivering value to their customer, the goal of process improvements and value additions have flown down to each and every individual employee working for the organization. As a result, not only the organization's success, but also the individual's success in terms of growth today heavily depend upon the value they deliver and the improvements they implement in the processes and products for the customer.

Today employees know that they need to deliver value, however due to the already tight deadlines they are expected to meet and their ever-increasing workload, their focus towards improvement projects and value additions tend to take a lower priority. This is especially true as the quality of the documentation required to execute process improvements in the form of six sigma projects, lean projects and PDCA projects is much high. And many times, they are unclear as what exactly should the content of the documents be.

This impacts their individual contribution towards process

improvements, and hence their growth, which in turn also impacts the overall business growth.

PDCA is an iterative four step method commonly used to continually control and improve processes and products.

This book is aimed at enabling businesses and their employees execute PDCA projects seamlessly and effectively, focusing only on the critical components, which will ensure a successful PDCA project execution.

# WHAT THIS BOOK AIMS TO HELP YOU WITH

This book aims to help you with the following,

➤ Explain the core essential components needed to execute a PDCA project.
➤ Explain how to execute a PDCA project, using the core essential components.
➤ Cover the above in least number of words possible – to help you deliver a PDCA faster.

However, please note that this book does not aim to

➤ Make you an expert in the Deming's PDCA cycle – your organization expects you to deliver PDCA projects faster, so we will keep our focus to that.

# PDCA

**P**DCA **(Plan–Do–Check–Act)** is an iterative four step method used for the control and continual improvement of processes and products. It is also known as the Deming cycle or the Shewhart cycle.

**Plan** – Involves assessing the process that needs to be improved, or a new process that needs to be developed. It focusses on brainstorming ways to improve the process and put up an improvement plan.

**Do** – Involves executing the established plan. Collecting the data to study the effectiveness of the change, developing and testing the improvement solution.

**Check** – Involves analyzing the collected data, evaluating and comparing against the established standards or the target.

**Act** – Involves baselining and establishing the new improved process, if the Check phase confirms the improvement. If on the other hand, the Check phase fails to confirm the improvement, then it involves either initiating a new PDCA cycle, or implementing necessary fixes in the improved process. If not anything, the old process itself also can be continued.

# PDCA – THE ESSENTIAL COMPONENTS

The essential components of a PDCA project are,

**PLAN**
- ➤ Charter
  - Business Case
  - Problem Statement
  - Goal Statement
  - Scope
  - Project Team
  - Timelines
- ➤ AS IS Data
- ➤ Plan Solution

**DO**
- ➤ Develop and Test Solution
- ➤ TO BE Data

**CHECK**
- ➤ Data Review

➢ Realization

**ACT**
➢ Action Plan
➢ Future Milestones

# PLAN ESSENTIAL COMPONENTS

The essential components of a Plan phase are,

**PLAN**
- ➢ Charter
  - • Business Case
  - • Problem Statement
  - • Goal Statement
  - • Scope
  - • Project Team
  - • Timelines
- ➢ AS IS Data
- ➢ Plan Solution

# CHARTER

**W**hat it is – A concise document that clearly describes the elements of the project by explaining the Business Case, the Problem, the Goal, the Scope, the Team and the Timelines of a project.

**Why is it important** – This is the most important component as it acts as a reference and a guide to manage and take the project to success.

# CHARTER

**H**ow to frame – Frame the Charter by including the following components,

➢ Business Case
➢ Problem Statement
➢ Goal Statement
➢ Scope
➢ Project Team
➢ Timelines

# BUSINESS CASE

**What it is** – A concise description of the improvement opportunity, explaining in brief the problem, the goal of the project, the reason why the project is important, along with financial justification if any for the execution of the project, and most importantly what is the negative impact, if the project is not executed right now.

**Why is it important** – This is the most important component as it enables the sponsor of the project to decide whether he can approve the particular opportunity for execution, over other potential improvement opportunities.

# BUSINESS CASE

**H**ow to frame – Frame the Business Case with a view to answer the following questions,

➤ What is the problem, the PDCA project is trying to solve or improve, what is the business opportunity?
➤ Where and with what frequency is the problem occurring?
➤ What is the financial impact of the problem?
➤ What is the business value of executing the PDCA project?
➤ What is the impact or risk of not utilizing the business opportunity right now?

Take approval from sponsor on the Business Case before you proceed.

# BUSINESS CASE

## Points to note

➤ Avoid mentioning the solution in the Business Case.
➤ Avoid giving any hint towards the solution in the Business Case.
➤ Avoid having exact same text in the Business Cases as in Problem and Goal statements; though they are related, they are not same.
➤ Ensure the impact of not executing the PDCA project right now, is mentioned.
➤ Ensure financial benefits of executing the project is mentioned in the Business Case.

# BUSINESS CASE

## Example

**Business Case:**

"ABC Business's XYZ Support Team performs daily monitoring, reporting user activity on XYZ system.

The report captures the details of daily active users on the XYZ system, including their ID, name, 'Last Activity Date' and 'Role'.

➤ The XYZ support team fetches details required for the report.
➤ Creates an excel report.
➤ And sends to the Business lead.

Daily there are at least around 50 active users for whom the data needs to be fetched.

Fetching the details, formatting the data into an excel report, and sending to the Business Lead takes around 2 hours daily, amounting to 47,450 USD annually.

This project aims at reducing this manual effort wastage by at least 80% and achieving a dollar saving of at least 37960 USD.

If this project is not initiated right now, it will result in continued wastage of effort and productivity"

# PROBLEM STATEMENT

**W**hat it is – A concise description of the problem or the issue or the condition which the PDCA project focusses to improve.

**Why is it important** – This is an important component as it helps identify the gap between the current and desired states of a process or product. This basically helps the team understand why the PDCA project is being done.

# PROBLEM STATEMENT

**How to frame** – Frame the Problem Statement with a view to answer the following questions related to the problem, the PDCA project is trying to fix or improve,

- ➢ What is the problem the PDCA project is trying to solve or improve?
- ➢ Where is the problem occurring?
- ➢ When does the problem occur and with what frequency?
- ➢ What is the financial impact of the problem?

# PROBLEM STATEMENT

## $\mathbf{P}$oints to note

- ➤ Avoid mentioning the solution in the Problem Statement.
- ➤ Avoid giving any hint towards the solution in the Problem Statement.
- ➤ Avoid having exact same text in the Business Case as in Problem statement; though they are - related, they are not same.
- ➤ Ensure financial impact of the problem is mentioned in the Problem Statement.
- ➤ Usually the Problem statement will have a more detailed description of the problem than the Business Case.

# PROBLEM STATEMENT

# Example

## Problem Statement:

"ABC Business's XYZ Support Team performs daily monitoring, reporting user activity on XYZ system.

The report captures the details of daily active users on the XYZ system, including their ID, name, 'Last Activity Date' and 'Role'.

- ➢ The XYZ support team fetches the users active within the last 24 hour, along with their 'ID', and 'Name' from the XYZ system log database.
- ➢ Then it fetches 'Last Activity Date' for all these active users from XYZ system.
- ➢ And 'Role' from the company employee data source.
- ➢ The XYZ team then puts the data into an excel file, formats it.
- ➢ And then emails this excel report to the Business Lead.

Daily there are around 50 active users for whom the data needs to be fetched.

Fetching the details from multiple sources and formatting the data into an excel takes around 2 hours daily.

This amounts to 47,450 USD annually at 65 USD hourly rate, and is a huge expense and productivity loss."

# GOAL STATEMENT

**W**hat it is – A concise description of the goal or the aim or the desired state which the PDCA project focusses to achieve within a specified period of time.

**Why is it important** – This is an important component as it helps identify the desired state of a process or product. It also helps identify the improvement target, and the deadline for the project.

# GOAL STATEMENT

**H**ow to frame – Frame the Goal Statement with a view to answer the following questions related to the aim of the PDCA project,

➢ What is the PDCA project targeting to improve?
➢ By how much percent is the PDCA project targeting to improve, that what it aims to improve?
➢ By when is the PDCA project targeting to improve, that what it aims to improve?
➢ What would the financial benefits be?

Overall the goal statement needs to be SMART (Specific, Measurable, Attainable, Relevant, Timebound)

# GOAL STATEMENT

## Points to note

- Start with a verb.
- Ensure to mention what the project aims to improve.
- Ensure to include the target in terms of percentage improvement.
- Ensure the timeline is mentioned.

# GOAL STATEMENT

# Example

## Goal Statement:

"Reduce the manual effort spent creating the daily activity monitor report by at least 80% by 30th June 2018, resulting in annual saving of at least 37960 USD"

# SCOPE

**W**hat it is – A concise description clearly demarcating what is in scope and what is out of scope of the PDCA project.

**Why is it important** – This is an important component as it helps to keep the team focused, and to set clear expectations for the stakeholders.

# SCOPE

**H**ow to frame – Frame the Scope with a view to answer the following questions for the PDCA project,

➢ What is in scope for the PDCA project?
➢ What is NOT in scope for the PDCA project?

Following are some of the things that can be scoped,

➢ Users
➢ Geographies
➢ Sub businesses
➢ Product features
➢ Time

# SCOPE

## **P**oints to note

➢ Sometimes it is enough to only include the In-scope, as anything out of In-scope will anyway be considered out of scope.

# SCOPE

# Example

## Scope:

In scope:

ABC Business
XYZ system Daily Monitoring Report

Out scope:

Anything beyond

# PROJECT TEAM

**What it is** – A concise description clearly mentioning the roles, and names of the people involved and necessary for the successful execution of the PDCA project.

**Why is it important** – This is an important component as it helps define the project team, their roles, and any other important stakeholders.

# PROJECT TEAM

**H**ow to frame – Frame the Project Team with a view to answer the following questions related to the people, involved in the PDCA project,

➢ Who are the members of the team?
➢ Who are the important stakeholders?
➢ What are their roles?

Following are some of the things that can be covered,

➢ Mentors
➢ Sponsor
➢ Project Lead
➢ Development Team
➢ Testing Team
➢ Deployment Team

# PROJECT TEAM

## Points to note

➢ Do remember to mention the Sponsor.
➢ Projects normally have BB mentor and MBB mentor, ensure to mention them.
➢ Sometimes there is an alternate lead along with the primary lead, mention them both.
➢ Capture details of any other important stakeholders.

# PROJECT TEAM

## Example

Project Team: GB – Suneet Karande
Sponsor – Sahana KS
MBB – Sumeet Savant

# TIMELINES

**W**hat it is – A concise description clearly mentioning the timelines needed for completion of the entire project, as well as for each phase of the PDCA project.

**Why is it important** – This is an important component as it helps keep the team focused, and to set clear expectations for the stakeholders.

# TIMELINES

**H**ow to frame – Frame the Timelines with a view to answer the following questions related to the planned schedule of the PDCA project,

➢ What are the timelines for execution of each of the phase of the PDCA project?

Following are some of the ways this can be presented,

➢ Activity Diagram
➢ Schedule Diagram
➢ Gant Chart
➢ Sequence Diagram
➢ Simple Table

Gant Chart is the preferred tool used for drawing the timelines in a PDCA project.

# TIMELINES

## Points to note

➢ The timelines need to stand out clearly for the phases.
➢ Care needs to be taken to ensure correct representations in case of diagrams.

# TIMELINES

# Example

**Timelines:**

PLAN Start Date – 16th April 2018
PLAN End Date – 30th April 2018

DO Start Date – 1st May 2018
DO End Date – 31st May 2018

CHECK Start Date – 1st June 2018
CHECK End Date – 15th June 2018

ACT Start Date – 16th June 2018
ACT End Date – 30th June 2018

# AS IS DATA

**W**hat it is – A concise description describing the performance of the AS IS process derived from the data collected.

**Why is it important** – This is an important component as it helps to understand the current or AS IS performance.

# AS IS DATA

**How to frame** – Frame the AS IS Data with a view to answer the following questions,

➤ What is the performance of the current process, before implementing the solution?

Use appropriate sampling mechanism and collect a representative data sample from the data population. Some of the common sampling techniques are,

➤ Probability Sampling
- Simple Random Sampling
- Stratified Sampling
- Cluster Sampling
- Systematic Sampling

➤ Non-probability Sampling
- Volunteer sampling
- Haphazard sampling

Some of the common data types are,

➢ Qualitative
- Binary
- Unordered
- Ordered

➢ Quantitative
- Continuous
- Discrctc

Tabulate the data collected.

# AS IS DATA

## **P**oints to note

➢ Choose appropriate sampling mechanism – sample should be representative of population.
➢ Choose appropriate data type.
➢ Avoid fake data, actually collect the data.
➢ Most importantly, clearly mention what is collected.

# AS IS DATA

# Example

**AS IS Data:**

Effort in minutes to fetch data and prepare report manually
(Mean) - 120 minutes

## AS IS Data Table

| Reading No. | Effort in minutes to fetch data and prepare report |
|---|---|
| 1 | 120 |
| 2 | 118 |
| 3 | 119 |
| 4 | 121 |
| 5 | 122 |
| 6 | 123 |
| 7 | 121 |
| 8 | 120 |
| 9 | 119 |
| 10 | 120 |
| 11 | 117 |
| 12 | 123 |
| 13 | 122 |
| 14 | 119 |
| 15 | 120 |
| 16 | 122 |
| 17 | 119 |
| 18 | 117 |
| 19 | 120 |
| 20 | 118 |
| 21 | 119 |
| 22 | 120 |
| 23 | 123 |
| 24 | 120 |
| 25 | 125 |

# PLAN SOLUTION

**What it is** – A concise description clearly explaining the designs and test cases, along with other considerations and plans to develop and test the solution.

**Why is it important** – This is one of the most important component as it helps to plan for the solution.

# PLAN SOLUTION

**How to frame** – Frame the Plan Solution with a view to answer the following questions,

➢ What are the design considerations for the solution?
➢ What are the test cases planned to test the correct and expected working of the solution?

These can be answered in a diagrammatic or text formats. Following are some of the design considerations that can be included,

➢ Frameworks
➢ Development Model
➢ Standards

Following are some of the diagrams that can be used,

➢ Architecture Diagram
➢ Block Diagram
➢ Component Diagram
➢ Process Map

➢ Data Flow Diagram
➢ Entity Relationship Diagram
➢ Mockup
➢ Network Diagram
➢ Sequence Diagram
➢ Use Case Diagram

Process Map and Flow Diagrams are preferred for PDCA projects.

Some of the common testing techniques are,

➢ Unit Testing
➢ Integration Testing
➢ Regression Testing
➢ Smoke Testing
➢ Alpha Testing
➢ Beta Testing
➢ System Testing
➢ Stress Testing

Before designing the solution, root cause identification using Fish Bone diagram can also be performed.

The Plan Solution can also include following plans,

➢ Implementation plan
➢ Deployment plan
➢ Roll back plan

# PLAN SOLUTION

## Points to note

➤ While including diagrams take care of data security constraints, like exclusion of IP addresses, usernames and passwords etc.
➤ Ensure the diagrams are easy to understand and comprehend.

# PLAN SOLUTION

# Example

**Plan Solution:**

## Solution Design Flow Diagram

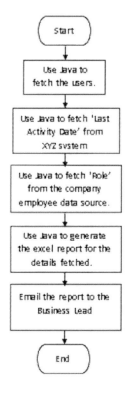

# DO ESSENTIAL COMPONENTS

The essential components of a Do phase are,

➢ Develop and Test Solution
➢ TO BE Data

# DEVELOP AND TEST SOLUTION

**W**hat it is – A concise description clearly explaining the process to develop and test the solution, on the basis of the design, and the tests planned in the PLAN phase.

**Why is it important** – This forms the core component, as it helps to develop and test the actual solution.

# DEVELOP AND TEST SOLUTION

**How to frame** – Frame the Develop and Test Solution with a view to answer the following questions,

➤ What are the cases tested to confirm the correct and expected working of the solution, based on the design developed in the PLAN phase?
➤ Has the sign-off on correct working of the solution taken from the users?

It is a good idea to do a Beta release if possible and get a UAT done from the Business Users.

# DEVELOP AND TEST SOLUTION

## **P**oints to note

➤ A low level design can also be created before development.
➤ Ensure all test cases planned are tested and tabulated.
➤ Ensure signoff from appropriate users is obtained on testing.

# DEVELOP AND TEST SOLUTION

# Example

**Develop and Test Solution:**

Sample Unit Test Cases Result Table

| Sl No. | Description | Expected Result | Observed Result |
|---|---|---|---|
| 1 | 'Last Activity Date' from XYZ system, and 'Role' from the company employee data is fetched for the users. | The details fetched should be accurate as present in the XYZ system and employee database | Same as Expected |

Sign off on the testing – Signed off by business owner dated 16th June 2018

# TO BE DATA

**W**hat it is – A concise description describing the performance of the TO BE process derived from the data collected.

**Why is it important** – This is an important component as it helps to understand the improved or the TO BE performance.

# TO BE DATA

**H**ow to frame – Frame the TO BE Data with a view to answer the following questions,

➢ What is the performance of the new process, after implementing the solution?

Use appropriate sampling mechanism and collect a representative data sample from the data population. Some of the common sampling techniques are,

➢ Probability Sampling
  - Simple Random Sampling
  - Stratified Sampling
  - Cluster Sampling
  - Systematic Sampling

➢ Non-probability Sampling
  - Volunteer sampling
  - Haphazard sampling

Some of the common data types are,

- ➤ Qualitative
  - Binary
  - Unordered
  - Ordered

- ➤ Quantitative
  - Continuous
  - Discrete

Tabulate the data collected.

# TO BE DATA

## **P**oints to note

➢ Choose appropriate sampling mechanism – sample should be representative of population.
➢ Choose appropriate data type.
➢ Avoid fake data, actually collect the data.
➢ Most importantly, clearly mention what is collected.

# TO BE DATA

# Example

**TO BE Data:**

Effort in minutes to fetch data and prepare report post automation (Mean) - 6.24 minutes

## TO BE Data Table

| Reading No.. | Effort in minutes to generate excel report |
|---|---|
| 1 | 7 |
| 2 | 6 |
| 3 | 6 |
| 4 | 7 |
| 5 | 8 |
| 6 | 7 |
| 7 | 5 |
| 8 | 6 |
| 9 | 5 |
| 10 | 6 |
| 11 | 5 |
| 12 | 7 |
| 13 | 6 |
| 14 | 5 |
| 15 | 6 |
| 16 | 7 |
| 17 | 6 |
| 18 | 6 |
| 19 | 7 |
| 20 | 6 |
| 21 | 7 |
| 22 | 6 |
| 23 | 7 |
| 24 | 6 |
| 25 | 6 |

# CHECK ESSENTIAL COMPONENTS

The essential components of a Check phase are,

➢ Data Review
➢ Realization

# DATA REVIEW

**W**hat it is – A concise description describing the comparison of the performance of AS IS and TO BE process based on the collected data, preferably in a visually enhanced manner.

**Why is it important** – This is an important component as it helps to evaluate the effectiveness and success of the executed PDCA. This will also help in deciding the concluding actions to be enacted in the ACT phase.

# DATA REVIEW

**H**ow to frame – Frame the Data Review with a view to answer the following questions,

➢ Did executing the PDCA project result in any performance improvement? Or was the original problem fixed

➢ If yes, how much has the performance improved?

Graph the AS IS and TO BE data in a chart, which will help to visualize the improvements that resulted from execution of the PDCA project.

Any of the following charts can be used,

➢ Bar Charts
➢ Column Charts
➢ Line Charts

However, bar charts are the preferred PDCA tool.

# DATA REVIEW

# **P**oints to note

➢ Choose clustered or stacked charts to bring out the difference in performance of the AS IS and TO BE processes effectively.
➢ Ensure the comparison is clear.

# DATA REVIEW

# Example

## Data Review:

PDCA project resulted in an improvement - Yes

Improvement achieved –

Effort Before PDCA - 120 minutes
Effort After PDCA - 6.24 minutes
Effort Reduction Achieved - 94.8% i.e. 113.76 min saved

## AS IS vs TO BE Chart

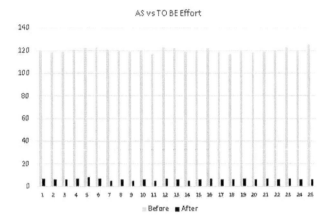

# REALIZATION

**W**hat it is – A concise description clearly explaining the achievements of the executed PDCA project.

**Why is it important** – This is an important component as it helps to summarize the overall achievements of the executed PDCA project.

# REALIZATION

**How to frame** – Frame the Realization with a view to answer the following questions,

- ➢ What are the financial benefits achieved as a result of executing the PDCA project?
- ➢ What are the Performance Improvements achieved as a result of executing the PDCA project?
- ➢ What are the other benefits achieved as a result of executing the PDCA project?

# REALIZATION

## Points to note

➢ Ensure the performance improvements are mentioned in same units, for example if AS IS data is calculated in person hours, then TO BE also should be in person hours.

➢ Remember to calculate and mention the annual dollar savings achieved.

➢ Mention any other parameters and benefits achieved appropriate for the executed PDCA project.

# REALIZATION

# Example

**Realization:**

Effort saved from 120 minutes to 6.24 minutes i.e. 94.8%.

Annual dollar spent before PDCA: 120 minutes * 365 days * 65 USD/60 minutes = 47450 USD

Annual dollar spent after PDCA: 6.24 minutes * 365 days * 65 USD/60 minutes = 2467.4 USD

Annual dollar saving achieved: 47450 USD – 2467 USD = 44983 USD

# ACT ESSENTIAL COMPONENTS

The essential components of an Act phase are,

➢ Action Plan
➢ Future Milestones

# ACTION PLAN

**What it is** – A concise description clearly explaining the plan of action devised in the ACT phase based on the achievements and realization summarized in the CHECK phase.

**Why is it important** – This is an important component as it helps to define the actions to be taken which can be either the steps taken to establish the developed solution as the new baseline, or to initiate a new PDCA project, or to fix the developed solution to use it as the new baseline.

# ACTION PLAN

**How to frame** – Frame the Action Plan with a view to answer the following questions,

➢ What are the identified actions to be performed in the ACT phase?

This can be either of the following,

➢ The steps to establish the developed solution as the new baseline.
➢ The steps to initiate a new PDCA project.
➢ The steps to fix the developed solution to use it as the new baseline.

Take sign off from the Sponsor for the success of the PDCA project.

# ACTION PLAN

## Points to note

➢ Let it be concise and crisp, with as many less words as possible.

➢ Preferred option is to use the developed solution as a new baseline.

➢ Avoid choosing to fix the solution to be able to use as a new baseline, as much as possible. Use this only as the last resort, prefer initiating a new PDCA cycle instead.

# ACTION PLAN

## $E$xample

**Action Plan:**

➢ Educate the XYZ team to use new solution by 30th June 2018.
➢ Inform all stakeholders about the new baselined process by 30th June 2018.
➢ Stop the old process and start using the new process by 1st July 2018.

# FUTURE MILESTONES

**W**hat it is – A concise description clearly explaining any future milestones of new projects arising out of the executed PDCA project.

**Why is it important** – This is an important component as it helps identify any new projects as a byproduct of the executed PDCA project.

# FUTURE MILESTONES

**How to frame** – Frame the Future Milestones with a view to answer the following questions,

➢ Will there be any next project(s) executed in continuation to the current one?
➢ What is the the need for next project(s)?
➢ What is the next project(s) about?
➢ What are the timelines for the next project(s)?
➢ Who are the important stakeholders and the team required for the next project(s)?

The need for the next project can come up for a number of reasons, some of them are listed below,
➢ In case the PDCA project executed was successful, then there might be plans of implementing the next version of the solution.
➢ In case the PDCA itself was a successful pilot, then a complete project may have to be implemented.
➢ In case the PDCA project was a failure, then a new PDCA cycle may have to be initiated.

# FUTURE MILESTONES

## Points to note

➢　Try to utilize this section to assert the mindset of continuous improvement.
➢　These details may be tentative at the moment.

# FUTURE MILESTONES

## Example

**Future Milestones:**

Any next project(s) planned - Yes

Need for next project(s) - Continual Improvement

Description – Automation of the email notification step.

Timelines – End of August 2018

Important Stakeholders and Team – Same as current project.

# 4 BLOCKER

This is the summary of the executed PDCA project.

This covers all the important components of the entire PDCA cycle like,

- ➢ Problem and Goal Statements.
- ➢ Timelines.
- ➢ Data Review.
- ➢ Realization.
- ➢ Action Plan.
- ➢ Future Milestones

# AUTHOR'S NOTE

I thank you for choosing the book, I have presented to you how exactly you can execute your Lean Six Sigma PDCA projects with the most essential components.

I hope this adds value to you and helps you execute a good number of Lean Six Sigma PDCA projects easily.

**Please leave a review on Amazon** or wherever you bought the book, and it will help me in my quest to provide good useful products to you on Lean Six Sigma.

All the very best,

Sumeet Savant
Lean Six Sigma Master Black Belt and Coach

Printed in Great
Britain
by Amazon